DIPLODOCUS

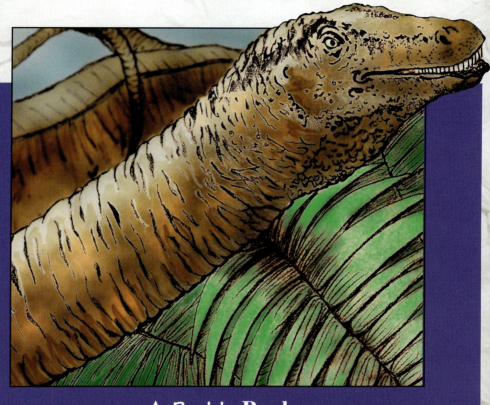

A Buddy Book
by
Michael P. Goecke

ABDO
Publishing Company

VISIT US AT
www.abdopub.com

Published by ABDO Publishing Company, 4940 Viking Drive, Edina, Minnesota 55435. Copyright © 2002 by Abdo Consulting Group, Inc. International copyrights reserved in all countries. No part of this book may be reproduced in any form without written permission from the publisher.

Printed in the United States.

Edited by: Christy DeVillier
Contributing editor: Matt Ray
Graphic Design: Denise Esner, Maria Hosley
Cover Art: Deborah Coldiron, title page
Interior Photos/Illustrations: page 5: Oil painting by Josef Moravec; pages 8, 9, 10, 11, 23 & 25: Deborah Coldiron; page 13 & 21: ©Douglas Henderson from *Riddle of the Dinosaurs* by John Noble Wilford, published by Knopf; page 15: M. Shiraishi ©1999 All Rights Reserved; page 17: Patrick O'Brien; page 27: courtesy of Friends of Dinosaur Ridge, Morrison, Colorado.

Library of Congress Cataloging-in-Publication Data

Goecke, Michael P., 1968-
    Diplodocus/Michael P. Goecke.
       p. cm. – (Dinosaurs set II)
    Includes index.
    Summary: Describes the physical characteristics and behavior of the long-necked Diplodocus.
    ISBN 1-57765-633-4
    1. Diplodocus—Juvenile literature. [1. Diplodocus. 2. Dinosaurs.] I. Title.

QE862.S3 G64 2002
567.913—dc21

2001027928

TABLE OF CONTENTS

What Were They? 4

How Did They Move? 8

Why Was It Special? 10

Where Did It Live? 12

Who Else Lived There? 14

What Did They Eat? 18

Who Were Their Enemies? 20

Family Life 22

The Family Tree 24

Discovery 26

Where Are They Today? 28

Fun Dinosaur Web Sites 30

Important Words 31

Index 32

WHAT WERE THEY?

The Diplodocus was one of the longest dinosaurs. It lived about 150 million years ago. That was during the late Jurassic period.

Diplodocus
Di-PLO-duh-kus

The Diplodocus was about 90 feet (27 m) long. That is longer than two school buses standing end to end.

The Diplodocus was a sauropod dinosaur. Some people call sauropods "long necks." The Diplodocus's neck was 26 feet (8 m) long.

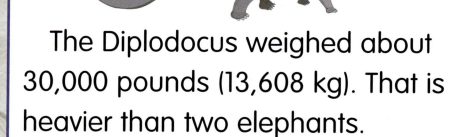

The Diplodocus weighed about 30,000 pounds (13,608 kg). That is heavier than two elephants.

How did they move?

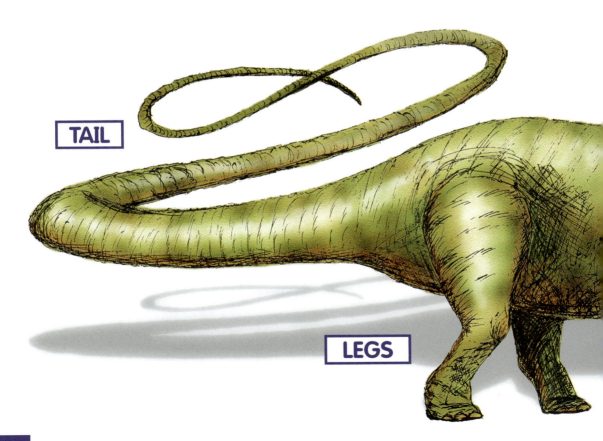

TAIL

LEGS

The Diplodocus walked on all four legs. It held its tail straight behind it. It could not raise its head very high. This dinosaur was too big to move very fast.

WHY WAS IT SPECIAL?

The Diplodocus had a very long tail. This tail was thin on the end. The Diplodocus may have used this tail like a whip. Maybe it fought other dinosaurs with this tail.

The Diplodocus's teeth were shaped like long spoons. They lay flat in its mouth. These flat teeth were good for tugging at plants.

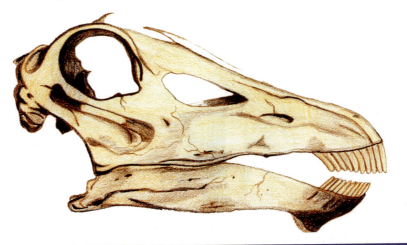

WHERE DID IT LIVE?

The Diplodocus lived in what is now North America. Canada, the United States, and Mexico make up North America.

Fossils show that the Diplodocus traveled together in herds, or groups. These herds moved through western North America looking for food. These plant-eaters found plenty to eat there.

The Diplodocus lived together in herds.

WHO ELSE LIVED THERE?

The Diplodocus lived among other sauropods. Two of these "long-necks" were the Apatosaurus and the Brachiosaurus. They had long tails like the Diplodocus. These "long-necks" probably traveled together in herds.

■ Brachiosaurus
■ Diplodocus
■ Apatosaurus

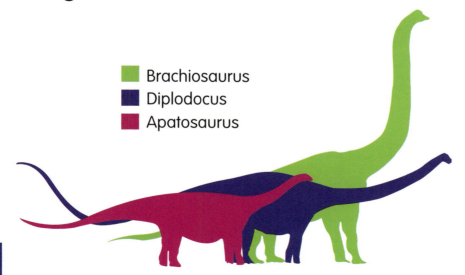

The Brachiosaurus was a sauropod.

The Diplodocus lived near the Stegosaurus, too. This plant-eating dinosaur had plates on its back. These plates were made of bone. We call these bone plates osteoderms.

The Stegosaurus had bone plates on its back.

WHAT DID THEY EAT?

The Diplodocus probably ate ferns and horsetail plants. These plants had soft leaves. It swallowed these leaves whole. The Diplodocus did not chew.

The Diplodocus also ate stones. We call these stones gastroliths. These gastroliths broke down the plants in the Diplodocus's stomach.

Ferns of today.

WHO WERE THEIR ENEMIES?

An adult Diplodocus was bigger than most animals. It was safe from enemies most of the time.

The young Diplodocus was small. It was not safe. It hid in forests. Meat-eaters like the Allosaurus may have hunted the young Diplodocus.

Meat-eaters did not hunt the giant Diplodocus very much.

FAMILY LIFE

The Diplodocus laid eggs in a circle on the ground. These eggs were as big as footballs. After hatching, the babies hid together in the woods. The Diplodocus did not raise its young.

Diplodocus babies hatched from eggs.

THE FAMILY TREE

The Vulcanodon was a sauropod. This "long neck" lived millions of years before the Diplodocus. Some people think it was the first sauropod.

The Vulcanodon was smaller than the Diplodocus. It was only 20 feet (6 m) long. It weighed about 8,000 pounds (3,628 kg).

The Vulcanodon

Discovery

Samuel W. Williston and Earl Douglass were fossil hunters. They discovered Diplodocus fossils in 1877. They worked for Othniel Marsh. He is a famous paleontologist. Othniel Marsh named the Diplodocus.

Williston and Douglass found these Diplodocus fossils at Dinosaur Ridge. This is in Morrison, Colorado. People have found many dinosaur fossils at Dinosaur Ridge.

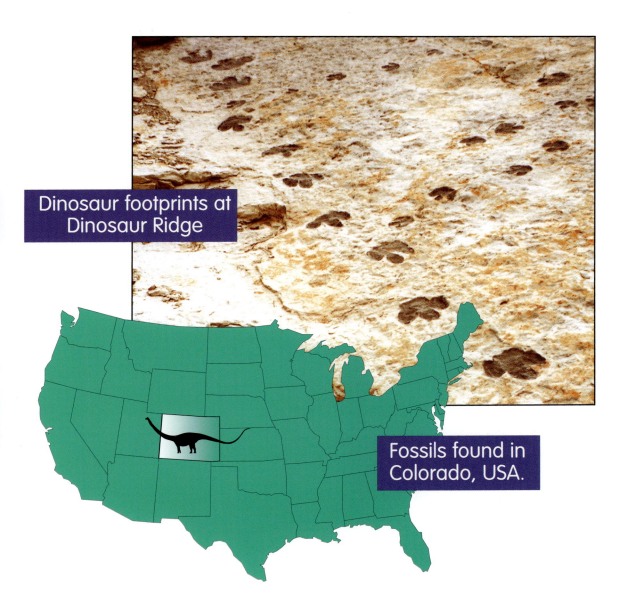

Dinosaur footprints at Dinosaur Ridge

Fossils found in Colorado, USA.

Where Are They Today?

Smithsonian National Museum of Natural History
10th Street and Constitution Avenue
Washington, D.C. 20560
www.nmnh.si.edu/paleo/dino

American Museum of Natural History
Central Park West at 79th Street
New York, NY 10024
www.amnh.org

Carnegie Museum of Natural History
4400 Forbes Avenue
Pittsburgh, PA 15213
www.clpgh.org/cmnh

London Natural History Museum
Cromwell Road
London, England SW7 5BD, UK
www.nhm.ac.uk/

DIPLODOCUS

NAME MEANS	Double-beamed
DIET	Plants
WEIGHT	20,000 - 40,000 pounds (9,071 - 18,144 kg)
LENGTH	90 feet (27 m)
TIME	Late Jurassic Period
ANOTHER SAUROPOD	Vulcanodon
SPECIAL FEATURE	Whip-like tail
FOSSILS FOUND	USA—Colorado, Wyoming, Utah, and Montana

The Diplodocus lived 150 million years ago.

First humans appeared 1.6 million years ago.

Triassic Period	Jurassic Period	Cretaceous Period	Tertiary Period
245 Million years ago	208 Million years ago	144 Million years ago	65 Million years ago

Mesozoic Era   Cenozoic Era

FUN DINOSAUR WEB SITES

Dinosaurs
www.cfsd.k12.az.us/~tchrpg/Claudia/Diplo.html
This web site contains basic information on the
Diplodocus, including its behavior and habitat, and
activities for children.

Enchanted Learning.com
www.enchantedlearning.com/subject/dinosaurs/
dinos/Diplodocus.shtml
Learn how smart the Diplodocus was compared to other
dinosaurs. Read about what it ate and where it lived.

BBC Online – Walking with Dinosaurs
www.bbc.co.uk/dinosaurs/sci_focus/production2.shtml
Read about how the young Diplodocus lived and why
scientists believe the Diplodocus could only eat certain
foods.

IMPORTANT WORDS

dinosaur reptiles that lived on land 248-65 million years ago.

fossil remains of very old animals and plants.

fossil hunter someone who hunts for fossils.

gastroliths stones the Diplodocus ate to break down food in its stomach.

horsetail a non-flowering plant that has been around for 408 million years.

Jurassic period a period of time that happened 208-146 million years ago.

osteoderms bone plates on the Stegosaurus's back.

paleontologist a person who studies plants and animals from the past.

whip a rope-like tool used to strike something.

Index

Allosaurus, **20**

Apatosaurus, **14**

Brachiosaurus, **14, 15**

Canada, **12**

Colorado, **26, 27, 29**

Dinosaur Ridge, **26**

Douglass, Earl, **26**

eggs, **22, 23**

ferns, **18, 19**

fossil, **12, 26, 27, 29**

gastroliths, **18**

herd, **12-14**

horsetail, **18**

Jurassic period, **4, 29**

long neck, **7, 14, 24**

Marsh, Othniel, **26**

Mexico, **12**

North America, **12**

osteoderms, **16**

sauropod, **7, 14, 15, 24, 29**

Stegosaurus, **16, 17**

United States, **12, 29**

Vulcanodon, **24, 25, 29**

whip, **10, 29**

Williston, Samuel W., **26**